Logan the Lobster

Written by Gloria Barnett

Illustrated by Pam Clubb

Footprint to the Future

Logan the spiny lobster was a very happy lobster.

He lived in the sea with his mum and had lots of lobster friends to play with.

They all had ten legs, two long antennae and hard brown shells.

It was impossible to tell them apart as they all looked so alike.

One sunny day, Logan was playing in the shallow waters when a **big wave** washed him out of the sea and onto the beach.

The sun was shining very brightly and Logan got sooooooooooo hot, he felt dizzy and sick.

He got **so hot** his whole body turned bright red!

His mum found him and quickly carried him back into the water.

After a few hours of cooling down, he felt much better.

He didn't feel dizzy anymore.

But ... now he didn't look like all his lobster friends!

In fact, he looked very, very different.

His shell was no longer brown ... he had changed colour completely.

Logan looked around ... this was scary ...

Then he suddenly realised ...

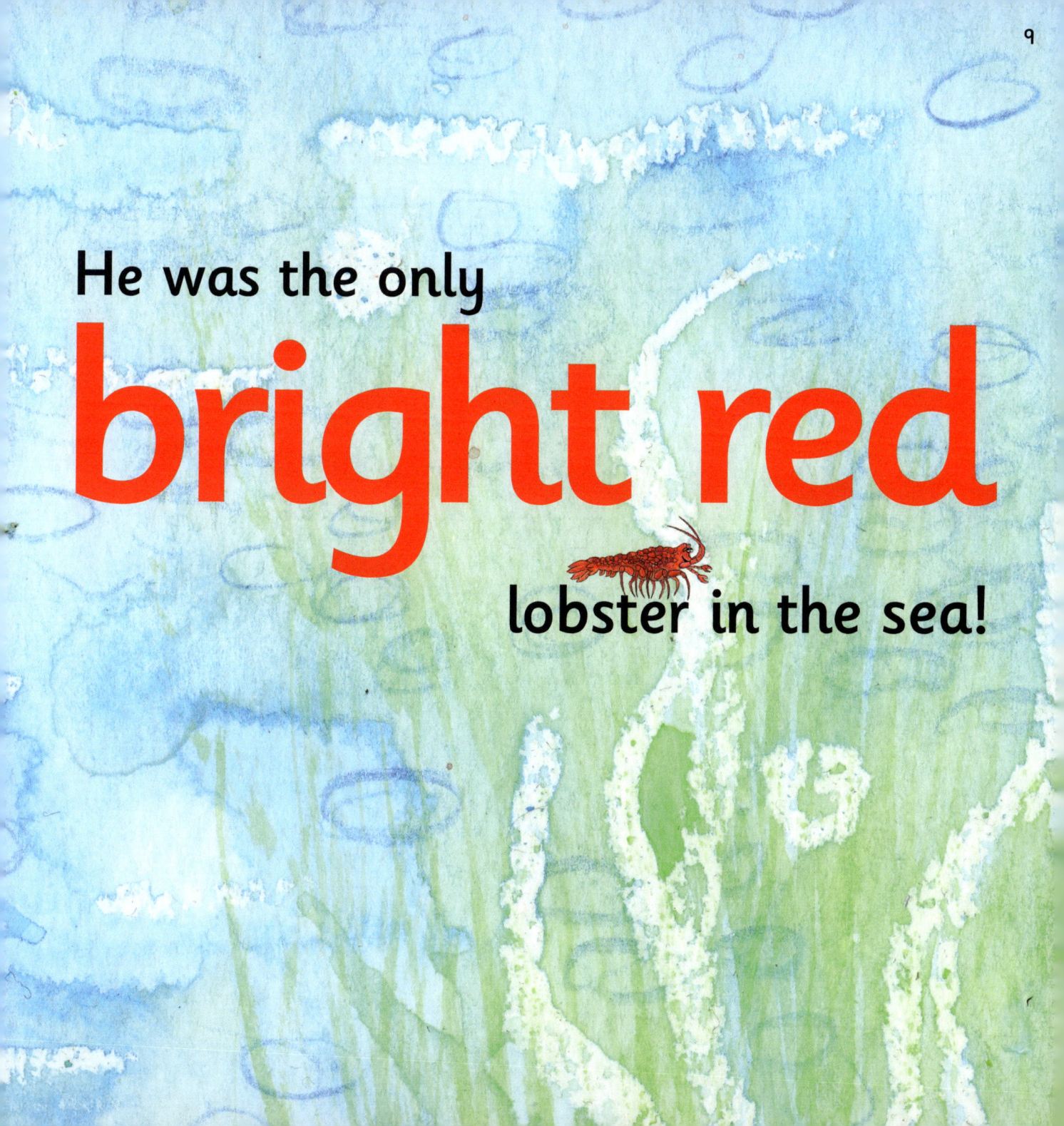

He was the only **bright red** lobster in the sea!

Poor Logan was very sad.
He didn't like being different.
He hid at home with his mum
so nobody would laugh at his bright red shell.

Early one morning a cloud of sand swept up from the seabed.
Logan heard a noise.
The noise had a beating rhythm, like the banging of a drum.

One, two ...
One, two ...
One, two.

The sound came closer ...
The sand started shaking ...
The beat became louder ...

The lobsters were marching away from the shallows, going to deeper, safer waters.

One, two … one, two … one, two …

Logan watched as big male lobsters marched at the front of the line, followed by females ... then at the back, hanging on tightly ... were the smallest lobsters.

They were all holding each other's tails and marching along one behind the other.

A massive line of lobsters was marching together.

The noise came from their stamping feet.

"Oh, Logan, quickly," he heard his Mum's voice,

"jump into the line …"

Was he brave enough to join the line?
Logan watched, then plucked up all his courage …

One … two … three … go!

He took some quick runny-type steps and jumped!

Yes, it worked!

He held onto the last lobster's tail and joined in the march.

The line of lobsters marched all day and all night, going deeper into the ocean.

When they stopped marching, they gathered around to listen to their leader.

Logan was told what the young lobsters did in the winter.
They all played football!
He got very excited. He loved football.

BUT will the other lobsters play with me?

The young lobsters chose teams and, because their shells were ALL brown, they made some colourful team shirts by wrapping their shells in soft coral.

There were lots of different coloured corals on the beautiful deep reef to choose from.

One team used green coral, whilst another team chose purple. Other teams wore pink, white, red and yellow colours.

But nobody chose Logan to be on their team.

He started to feel very sad … and was just about to crawl away behind the coral for a little cry when one of the young lobsters called out to him.

Logan was so happy!

He asked some slimy sea slugs to take turns to be the football.

The sea slugs loved it!

They would curl up in a ball and when the lobsters played with them, it didn't hurt a bit.

Logan could make a whistling noise with his mouth and when he blew his 'whistle', everyone played the game properly.

Soon **everyone** was having fun.

A few months later, everyone gathered around Logan and cheered.

He'd been the referee for every game, and they all said thank you for his hard work.

"Without you, Logan, we couldn't have had so much fun."

Now it was time to return to the shallow water.

They all lined up and held onto the tail in front.

This time Logan was in the middle of the line with his friends.

One, two …
one, two …
one, two …

they marched back to the warm shallow waters of the coral reef.

Logan had enjoyed his winter.

He now had lots of friends who loved him and his bright red shell.

Perhaps being different wasn't so bad after all.

SCIENCE STUFF ... DID YOU KNOW?
SPINY LOBSTERS

- Lobsters are crustaceans, related to crayfish, shrimps and crabs
- They have long bodies with muscular tails
- They moult in order to grow. This means they climb out of their shell, grow, and then make a new bigger shell to protect them
- Spiny lobsters are the only lobsters which migrate in the winter to deeper water
- Over 50 lobsters have been seen marching together
- They can live up to 70 years
- Lobsters are popular sea food and turn bright red when cooked
- Lobsters have blue blood
- They live in crevices of coral reefs, or burrows on the sea floor
- Spiny lobsters have no claws whilst other species of lobsters have two big pincher claws
- There are over 10,000 lobster species
- Lobsters lift their tail and run backwards if threatened

SCIENCE STUFF ... DID YOU KNOW?
CORAL REEFS

- Coral is an animal
- Reefs are made up of millions of different corals
- Corals are the largest natural structures in the world and can be seen from space

SCIENCE STUFF ... DID YOU KNOW?
SEA SLUGS

- Sea slugs are invertebrates - they have no backbone
- Sea slugs use gooey slime to help them to move over hard coral
- Sea slugs can't see well - they don't have eyes - just horn-like structures at the top of their head which can only 'see' light or dark
- Sea slugs have their lungs outside of their body. These are feathery looking organs which camouflage them amongst the colourful coral reefs
- Sea slugs absorb oxygen from the water through the feathery organs
- Sea slugs do not have gills like fish

OTHER TITLES BY THIS AUTHOR:

FISHY TALE STORYBOOKS
AGE 3-6

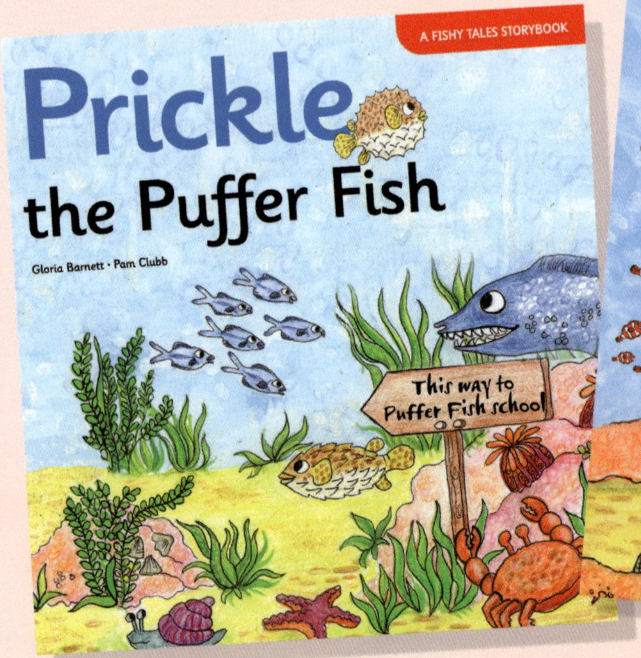

Prickle the Puffer Fish
A coral reef can be a very dangerous place to live. How can Prickle keep herself safe? Can she be brave?

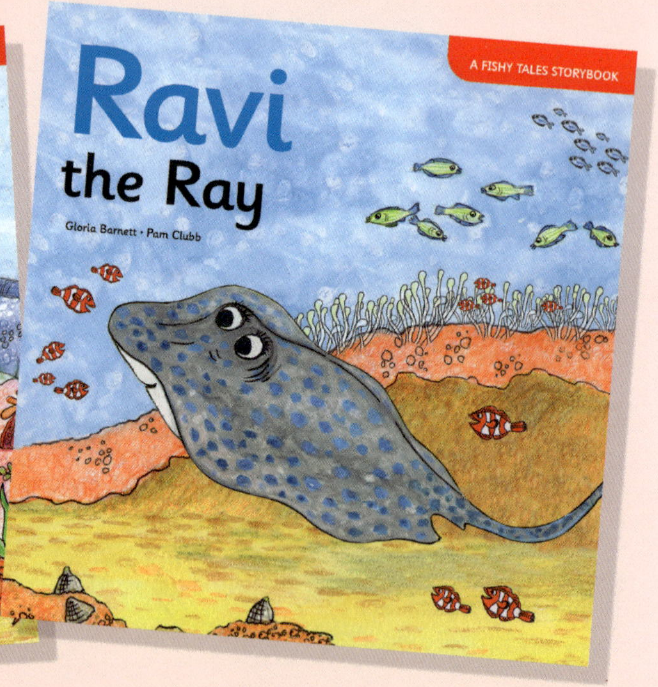

Ravi the Ray
Ravi is always on the move to keep out of danger. Can he find a settled home and friends to share his life with?